To Ann—
May all your Chr[istmases be ones]
of the heart!

Warmly,
Virginia T.
McAfee

A Season of the Heart

by
Virginia T. McAfee

A Season of the Heart

Copyright © 1995 by Virginia T. McAfee

All rights reserved. No part of this work may be reproduced in any way without the expressed written consent of the author, except in the form of brief excerpts or quotations for the purposes of review. Requests for permission should be addressed to Homeplace Books, Rt. 1, Box 1935, Wrightsville, Georgia 31096.

To order: send $12.95 plus $2.00 shipping and handling to:

> Homeplace Books
> Rt. 1, Box 1935
> Wrightsville, GA 31096

Printed in the United States of America

ISBN: 0-9647323-0-0

This book is dedicated to my mother for whom I am a first and only edition. She wisely edited my formative years, and her unconditional love continues to speak volumes.

Contents

A Season of the Heart *1*
Christmas Is ... *4*
Christmas Is Also... *7*
Christmas Snowfall *10*
The Magic of a Christmas Twilight *13*
Enjoying the Season *16*
Christmas: A Time of Affirmation *19*
Sweet Christmas Memories *23*
The Music of the Season *26*
Christmas at the Homeplace *29*
Seeking Peace *33*
Christmas Simplicity *36*
Christmas Recollections in a
   Country Church Yard *39*
Season of Celebration *42*
Christmas: A Season for Children *45*
The Perfect Tree *48*
Christmas Tree Lesson *52*
Timeless Charm *55*
Christmas Tree Memories *58*
No Carols the Second Time *61*

Contents *continued*

Christmas Tree Obsession *64*

Silent Night *67*

Christmas Music Charms the Savage Breast *70*

Windows at Christmas *73*

The Quiet Center *76*

Commercialism vs. Christmas *79*

Dear Santa *82*

Saying Farewell *86*

Preface

This collection of Christmas columns was written over a span of ten years for my local newspaper, the *Wrightsville Headlight*. Because Christmas is a complex season of anticipation and nostalgia, these columns reflect the joys as well as the introspection and, yes, patience this time of year brings. If the reader notices similarities in some of my thoughts, please be forgiving as my favorite parts of this *Season of the Heart* are those that never change.

Thank you to:

— Mary Eleanor Wickersham, former editor of The *Wrightsville Headlight*, and Robert Garrett, editor of the *Sandersville Progress*, for allowing me a place to share my thoughts over the last twelve years,

— Ray Irwin for her artistic advice,

— John Lounsbury and Mary Mitchell for turning my dream into a reality.

Virginia McAfee

A Season of the Heart

To capture Christmas in words is to imprison it in terms that become trite and predictable by their own limitations. I cannot capture Christmas in even one carol that escapes through stained glass windows and evaporates in the still winter air. Christmas is more than the simple cedar wreath hanging in classic beauty on a worn wooden door. Christmas defies even the magical beauty of myriads of white lights on store fronts and houses. Its true essence goes beyond the warm glow of candles burning in a quiet church or of trees decorated with memories handed down lovingly from one generation to the next.

Christmas wears many faces. It shines like new tinsel in the eyes of children dreaming of Santa Claus and busy elves. It simmers gently in the faces of the elderly as they remember other Christmases when their homes were filled with laughter and activity.

We have attempted to wrap Christmas in a festive package. We have put lights on it and bows and tinsel. We have written music in praise of it. We have created plays and pageants in honor of it. Christmas is something that cannot be explained by our tangible expressions of celebration. Christmas – the Christmas spirit – is something that begins in the quiet places of our heart and radiates into the cold world of reality around us.

We are spiritual beings always trying fruitlessly to quench a spiritual need with worldly things. The first Christmas happened, and the world has never been quite the same. We were offered an answer to hopelessness and pain that first Christmas, but the human condition in its complexity has received its greatest gift with an assortment of reactions these 2,000 years. Christmas is a reminder of who we are and of what we could and should be. Its complexity lies in its stark simplicity. We are human. We become caught up in a life of activity and stirring, stress and worry. We push ourselves looking for something, something that is more likely to come when we sit still and allow it to happen.

The first Christmas came quietly, unceremoniously. Great events and precious moments are usually greeted in silence, for no words can express our deepest feelings. Christmas comes but once a year, but for those who understand its silence and peace, it is here every day.

Christmas Is ...

Like the center of a burning candle is this season we call Christmas. Children bask in its glow and thrill to the light of a feeling that comes only one season a year. Older folk find pleasure and pain in the familiar intensity of emotions as they remember other seasons haunted by the ghosts of loved ones long gone and memories turned golden with the passing of time.

Christmas is light. It is upturned faces glowing with the excitement of the holiday. It is decorations twinkling through frosted window panes, the single taper in the modest window, the brilliant fire of a cathedral's stained glass. Christmas is translucent winter mornings, moonlight on untouched snow, gleaming frost that sews icicles on rooftops and quiet barns. It is the glow of a star on an evergreen; it is the glow of a star that burns brightly within each of us and still leads those who choose to seek peace and meaning in this fleeting life.

Christmas is warmth. It is the crackling fire beneath cedar garlands and holly boughs on wide mantles. It is the spicy contentment of steaming cocoa and hot Russian tea. It is woolen mittens pushed deep into coat pockets on brittle winter evenings. It is blankets and faded quilts piled high on beds cradling children sleeping away the nights while awaiting Santa's heralded arrival. Christmas is the warmth of friendships reaffirmed, acquaintances acknowledged, love restated. It is that best of times when emotions bubble gently, and we are allowed to skim the best of ourselves and give it freely, lovingly, unconditionally.

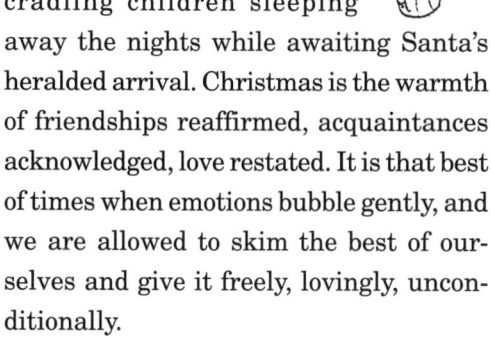

For some the Christmas season temporarily pushes aside the cold and darkness of reality and brings a warmth and light that comfort and sustain. For others the glow of the season serves only to make the dark corners of the soul appear even darker by contrast. Christmas, like the simple candle, starts with a tiny spark and burns steadily until its source of fuel is depleted. Christmas, unlike the candle, should be intangible. It should not be a material celebration but a celebration of the heart, a triumph of the soul.

Yes, Christmas is a season of light and warmth. May it be a season kindled by love, for love does not diminish as it is shared. It merely grows stronger as it pushes aside the cold and darkness of the human condition and reminds us of priorities and meaning and our reason for being.

Christmas Is Also ...

Christmas is the pungent smell of evergreen boughs in the winter air. It is the fragrant steam rising off spiced cider, wood smoke from an open fireplace framed in holly or pine, and peppermint pillows in a cut-glass jar in the living room. Christmas smells like warm candle wax in a quiet sanctuary, cookies and candy in decorative tins that recall a past era, and fresh fruit nestled in baskets made special with red velvet bows. Christmas is the smell of humanity as people gather in places of worship, social halls and homes to celebrate the season, their coats and hair holding their perfume or the scents of their separate households.

Christmas is the silver tinkling of tiny bells, the sonorous peal of chimes, the velvet harmony of human voices singing a timeless hymn of adoration. It is the uncomplicated music of children's laughter and the soft chuckle that slowly bubbles from older hearts that have experienced many holidays and now reminisce in the silence of their rooms. Christmas is pipe organs and guitars, majestic choirs and slightly off-key renditions of "Silent Night," the phone call made once a year, and the comfort of familiar voices gathered around the tree on Christmas Eve.

Christmas is red velvet and gold bows on garlands of cedar or pine. It is the breath of carolers on the night air, the pink cheeks of infants reflected in the ornaments of their first Christmas tree. It is the glitz of mall decorations and the simplicity of a single candle in the window of a modest home. Christmas is faces that glow with innocent joy or that turn pensive with recollections of the past. Christmas is white lights twinkling on a tree that goes all the way to the ceiling. It is new fallen snow on mountain peaks that echo only the low moan of a wintry wind.

Christmas tastes like hot chocolate and fruitcake, eggnog, homemade fudge and divinity, Mama's special casseroles, turkey, dressing, and cranberry sauce one more time, and popcorn puffs that didn't quite make it to the tree. Christmas leaves one's mouth dry in anticipation of the jolly old elf, and Christmas is the salty taste of tears at the sound of that special song or in the silence left by a beloved friend or family member whose presence is missed.

We can smell, hear, see, and taste Christmas, but we cannot touch it with our senses. Christmas can be felt only with our hearts. Christmas — the true meaning of the holiday — comes from deep within that part of us which is spiritual, universal, ethereal. In this season we see that which is most reverent and hope to define the greater meaning of our limited humanity in the answer. All the rest is mere decoration. The Christmas season is beautiful and poignant in all its earthly trappings, but its greatest message must be sought in the silence of the human heart which ultimately understands only the intangible and the ageless.

Christmas Snowfall

I watched the snow falling silently at midnight and marveled at the way it glistened like Christmas tinsel in the glow of our front porch light. Sometimes we are afraid to believe in miracles because we become vulnerable to disappointment. I wanted to believe that just once I might see snow at Christmas, and I held my breath for fear of breaking the spell as I watched downy flakes fall across the landscape.

The snow that was settling lightly into the dark spaces of nearby pastures and in the tiny cups of leaves would be as temporary as the holiday season. We could hope to enjoy it only a few magical hours before it would fade before our eyes and cause the world to return to normal. I chose, however, to savor the beauty of the moment rather than to fret over its brief duration. Like a child before a Christmas tree, I stood before an upstairs window and watched my world transform into something ethereal.

I had always wanted to experience the singular thrill of a white Christmas, but Christmas in Georgia could not even guarantee cold weather. I have spent the holiday in shorts and cotton blouses as well as in warm coats and gloves. A light dusting of snow worthy of mention usually came in February or March, if at all. Christmas weather usually meant overcast skies and a tenacious drizzle that turned crisp days raw and dreary.

Christmas lights shine more clearly against a backdrop of white. Candles glow more brightly, and red bows on front door wreaths stand out in sharper contrast when the world is blanketed in snow. Plastic Santas and snowmen look more believable, and the most modest home is transformed into something that is at once inviting and picturesque. Christmas scenes worthy of becoming the most elegant transcend the ordinary and become mystical in their untouched beauty.

Yes, we are often hesitant to believe that miracles, even small ones, can occur. Christmas is the season for miracles, and this year I received a Christmas wish. It

came a little late, but that part of
me that will remain a child welcomed it, nevertheless, and felt
no less joy in its arrival long
after I had first hoped for
snow at that most special
time of the year.

The Magic of
a Christmas Twilight

The sleet had finally stopped, but the sky sagged heavily and refused to give up its gray shroud as evening settled quietly over the pastures and woods on each side of the cold, frosted windows of my car. I had been Christmas shopping, and my last stop had made me late for my expected arrival home.

I knew that darkness would soon overtake me, so I slowed to a reasonable speed and decided to enjoy my solitary ride. The world was cold and wet — raw we would call it — but the interior of my car was warm and dry and comfortably crowded with paper sacks and boxes of gifts to be wrapped later. Seldom do I find myself alone. I momentarily missed my two young sidekicks who usually accompany me almost everywhere, but the magical hour of twilight drew my mind like a magnet to a private world of introspection.

As the woods and fields grew darker, I was reminded of how gray the world always appears at Christmas. We expect the cold and the rain and, ironically, resent balmy unseasonable weather during the holidays. Lights are brighter and fires are more inviting when the wind whips through brittle, bare trees and cold spikes of rain pierce winter's darkness.

I pushed in a tape of Christmas music, and familiar melodies filled the car and guided my thoughts back to other winter evenings when Christmas was full of the expectations of Santa Claus. That unique excitement comes vicariously now as I make the magic for my own children. A dull sadness tugged at me as I realized my older son would soon be too old to continue the dearest mystery of childhood.

My own childhood appeared in scenes as my mind jumped from one thought to another. Past Christmases were reviewed in visions that were at once painfully sharp and vaguely haunting. I remembered faces I missed acutely at this time of the year. I recalled events that grew more precious with each passing season and moments made more vivid by candlelight, Christmas tree lights, or the glow of smiles on the faces of loved ones.

I turned off the road I had traveled for several miles and rounded the curve that would lead me home. Darkness surrounded me. I was thirty minutes late. I had come a long distance, but not half so far as my memories had taken me in the magic of a Christmas twilight when the world was cold but the heart was warm and responsive.

Enjoying the Season

Sunday mornings usually mean that I can sleep a little longer, but I am up early this morning with only my thoughts to keep me company. The house is still, and I am filled with contentment as I sit by the Christmas tree that supplies my light in an otherwise dark room. I didn't know that it had rained last night, and it continues to rain now. The highway below my upstairs window glistens. The wet fields look a deeper brown. The stand of pines in the distance are a somber green. I sense the cold beyond my window.

Christmas is only days away now. Activities related to the holiday season are coming quickly, and I find that I cannot do all that I would like. I have bought most of my gifts and fulfilled several of my responsibilities. Some of the best is yet to come, and I anticipate the events of the next two weeks with joy.

I have not always felt so warmly about Christmas. When I became an adult, Christmas slowly began to symbolize the pressure of commitments, extra responsibilities, and exhaustion. This intense holiday was also a poignant reminder of past celebrations shared by loved ones who were no longer alive.

As the magic of childhood and Santa Claus grew dimmer, the realities of adulthood overshadowed much of the excitement I had once enjoyed at Christmas. I also grumbled about how soon after Thanksgiving the commercial world pushed Christmas upon us. That first Christmas display in late October or early November was more an omen of the mad rush ahead than a reminder of the beauty of the season.

I cannot explain the change. Perhaps it came because of my children. Perhaps I am a bit wiser than I was last year. At some point just before Thanksgiving, I decided I would sample all of the pleasures of the holidays without allowing myself to become tired and frustrated. I decided that memories are dear, but the present is no less precious. My children are forming their Christmas memories right now, and I owe it to them to make their childhood recollections as poignant as many of mine have been.

So, I shall enjoy the decorating, the programs, and even the crowds because I have reminded myself that I can stop whenever I wish and sit quietly beside my Christmas tree in the early morning silence. I remind myself, too, that I cannot bring back loved ones, but I can reminisce with happiness in the knowledge that I am presently forming memories for those lives I still share. This Christmas will be a memory very soon. It will be a special one for me because I allowed myself the peace and joy that Christmas should be if we remember why we celebrate and open our hearts to the true spirit of the season.

Christmas: A Time of Affirmation

My memories of past Christmases are like dreams – flashes, disjointed recollections, faint stirrings that do more to evoke emotions than visions. Christmas is a time of traditions. Its beauty and, yes, its pain lie in the fact that we once again turn our minds and especially our hearts, sometimes involuntarily, to seasons past. Almost reverently we display decorations whose beauty can sometimes be seen only by their owners – Santas with ragged beards and faded dress, nativity scenes with missing pieces, wreaths with wrinkled bows and long lost sprigs of holly berries. We decorate with these tangible memories that become dearer with each fleeting year.

Especially dear to me are my dime store decorations – the chipped ornaments, plastic Santas, glittering sleighs and reindeer purchased at a time when the big chain stores to which we now make our yearly pilgrimage were nonexistent.

The elegance of velvet wreaths, the opulence of light-strewn trees and bushes and the crude dignity of homemade nativity scenes are not without their places of importance during the season, but I remember a time of cedar gathering and simple handmade wreaths, a season of holly, mistletoe, and soft pine boughs bunched throughout the long hallway of the old homeplace. I fondly recall church programs with a baby doll infant, self-conscious shepherds in wool housecoats, towel-turbaned wisemen bearing foil-covered gifts, and sheet-draped angels topped with coat-hanger halos wound in tinsel.

Christmas is going to our little country church and singing carols that have echoed on cold winter nights through the ages. It is sitting on worn pews in candlelight and listening to that same story, knowing it by heart and yet hearing it for the first time.

Christmas is the reflection of unseen images on the faces of children – images that only a child can see and understand in his untouched innocence. It is expectations, surprises, joy. It is Santa Claus, Father Christmas, Père Noël, and Kris Kringel.

Christmas is loneliness. It is a reminder of changes that have taken place over the past year, of faces missing in the holiday crowd, of mistakes made, commitments still unfulfilled, and fears just over the horizon.

Christmas is celebration. It is anthems vibrating from the depths of mighty pipe organs and dissipating over hushed congregations. It is the carol played haltingly by hands that are long familiar with the old, slightly out-of-tune parlor piano. It is the extravagant party. It is the cup of tea and the afternoon conversation shared seasonally by dear friends.

Christmas is chocolate-covered cherries, fruitcake and ambrosia, peppermint sticks, and candy kisses. It is eggnog out of the carton and roast turkey with all the trimmings. Christmas is poinsettias, holly, evergreen trees, and mistletoe.

Above all else, Christmas is the proof that we are all individuals as we celebrate in our own ways, but from the greatest complexities arise the simplest truths – truths that sound trite when they are voiced because they are so well understood. We seek the same goals though sometimes through different routes. The miracle of Christmas leads us to the same end. It is not a miracle of the mind but of the heart and its needs. Like the child who needs to believe in Santa, the adult needs to believe also. We rejoice that our beliefs are not myths but a fact that the season – in its agony and its ecstasy – reaffirms.

Sweet Christmas Memories

I knew that Christmas was coming when Granddaddy brought home the candy. It wasn't just any candy. It was candy that was to be enjoyed only between Thanksgiving and Christmas. Assorted hard candies, soft peppermint sticks, and chocolate-covered cherries would appear magically and provide temptation for young taste buds that favored treasured sweets. Christmas has always been a season to thrill the senses. The clean, sharp fragrance of peppermint and the dark, rich smell of chocolate mingled pleasantly with the scent of fresh-cut pine and cedar that adorned mantles and table tops throughout the large homeplace.

Baking was a part of that season. Fruit cakes necessitated patience and skill as nuts had to be picked out and fruit had to be chopped by hand into small, even pieces before going into the rich, smooth batter. Walnuts and Brazil nuts, like the candy, appeared only during the holiday season and tempted even the most resolute willpower. Picking out the nuts for cakes and candy was not so much a tedious chore as it was a temptation to eat the results of one's efforts.

Fruit had been a special treat during my grandfather's childhood, and boxes of oranges and apples were another part of the holiday tradition at our house. Oranges tasted the sweetest when eaten in the warm glow of the Christmas tree. Apples were never cooler or crisper than when they were eaten in front of an inviting fire on a cold December night.

Memories are not always built upon dramatic events or sparkling fanfare. The best memories are pieced together lovingly like the scraps of an old quilt that will continue to warm long after we forget the history behind each carefully sewn bit of fabric. We remember parts, but when each part comes together, it forms a memory that is beautiful in its own right.

I cannot recall every Christmas I have ever experienced, but I remember bits and pieces – glowing Christmas trees, the aroma of spices filling every corner of the kitchen, the laughter of voices now silent, and my memories are sweet – as sweet as Granddaddy's candy.

The Music of the Season

I was no more than six when Mama and I began singing harmony. I carried the melody while she supplied the harmonizing notes that made me sound good. We did most of our singing at night on the way home from church or school programs, and our original repertoire consisted mostly of Christmas carols.

"Silent Night" and "Away in a Manger" were our favorites. The harmony was so close and the melodies so simple. I sat on my knees with my back against the car door, and I could look into the sky when I got to the parts about "all is calm, all is bright" and "The stars in the sky looked down where he lay." In my innocence I pictured a traditional manger scene on a cold, clear night like the ones just beyond the warmth of our car.

Christmas music has always cast a spell over me. From the simple chords of "Silent Night" to the ethereal sounds of Tchaikovsky's *Nutcracker Suite*, Christmas music sends a timeless and eloquent message to the listener. During no other season does music play such an important part in setting the mood or stirring the soul, and barely does the prelude begin, it seems, before the season ends.

Never is the world so drawn together than at Christmas when we sing carols that span decades and countries that, if at no other time, share a common bond. Modern audiences can still feel the magic of the sixteenth century in the sustained passages of "The Coventry Carol." From France the staccato rhythm of "Pat-A-Pan" serves as a model for our century's "Little Drummer Boy," and Germany's "O Christmas Tree" tells of the beloved tradition of decorating trees that originated in that country.

Christmas is a holiday for children, a celebration of one child, and many songs remind us of the real reason for Christmas trees and festivities. The simplicity of "O Come, Little Children," "The Friendly Beasts," and "Children Go Where I Send Thee" is ageless and moving. A power lies in innocence because each listener recognizes in himself the child who forever remains buried in our hopes and dreams only to emerge when we occasionally free ourselves of the pressures consistently present in the adult world.

I cherish my first memories of music. We need music in our lives to move those dark places within us into the light. We need Christmas music to define what mere words cannot. How does one explain joy, hope or need? How do we relay a powerful message to mankind when words are insufficient containers for the fullness of the story?

Music must be a part of my life, and Christmas music will always be special. I listen to it all year, not just during the holiday season because the message it brings cannot be limited to a few days in December. It is a message that needs to be heard all year long.

Christmas at the Homeplace

The living room at my homeplace was off limits to the children. It was a large, airy room with tall bay windows that curved around on the eastern wall at the front of the house and gave definition to the exterior of the big wooden structure.

The piano, a black upright, sat heavily on a thick wool rug that matched the large burgundy chairs and sofa that had held vigil there as long as I could remember. The cushions were needlepoint on a black velvet background and were sat upon only when the preacher came for dinner on Sunday or when the ladies of the community met for a baby shower or for a neighborhood social.

The dark tables smelled of furniture polish, and the shelves of books lining the built-in bookcase emitted a fascinating, musty fragrance that I equated with knowledge and importance. One of the doors was slightly loose on its hinges, and the fact that I was not allowed to open the wide glass doors made the books even more impressive.

The Christmas tree was placed in the living room as usual. The bay windows were a perfect setting, and we always had a large tree that stretched up toward the fourteen foot ceiling. I eagerly anticipated going into the woods with my grandfather to find the thickest pine or cedar, and we usually brought home a tree that was so big it had to be anchored in a silver lard bucket filled with wet sand. Size didn't matter. The room it would decorate was big enough for the most massive evergreen.

We had many decorations, but I remember best the bubble lights that perked silently in shades of red, green and gold and the garlands of tiny multicolored balls that had been purchased when my mother was a child. We never put an angel or star on our tree, but we filled the branches with ornaments and carefully placed icicles upon every bough from top to bottom.

Santa would visit this room. It had no heater, but a small fireplace by the bookshelves was used for the infrequent occasions when the room was occupied. The room was always cold on Christmas morning. We kept the door closed to shut the cold out of the rest of the house, and I can still recall the nip of fresh greenery on icy air when we opened the door to see what Santa had brought.

Childhood memories are often inexplicable even to the one remembering. I cannot recall many of the toys I received as a child nor many outstanding moments, but I always remember that seldom-used living room smelling of evergreen boughs and the polished furniture reflecting the warm glow of burning lights. I also still remember the initial excitement that quickened my pulse when I would open the door to see what Santa had delivered on each particular year.

Santa comes only once a year, and his visits are so few when one measures the length of a lifetime. Perhaps these memories have remained when others have faded because I was truly a child when the Christmas tree stood in that living room over thirty years ago. I would know other living rooms and other Christmases but never like those when Santa Claus and the magic of childhood were so wonderful and so real.

Seeking Peace

It was late – past bedtime on a school night – and we were all tired. Our fatigue, however, was the nice, peaceful kind that settles easily into sleep. The boys and I had been to a Christmas program at school, and now we were driving home, warmed by the glow of the Christmas spirit that had begun to surface as a result of the presentation we had just enjoyed.

Time is relative, and although the bedtime hours had come for my young sons, it was not too late for Christmas lights to be gleaming from the windows, roofs, and porches our car quietly passed. It was cool outside, and the humming warmth of the car heater began to lull my little ones to sleep. As they slept, their mother reminisced in the peace and warmth of the moment.

When I was their age, we lived in the country, and a special part of Christmas was driving to town to see the decorations.

Christmas did not come so early then. The moment of its arrival was more intense and exciting than it is now, or perhaps I see Christmas through adult eyes that do not shine quite so quickly or brightly as those of the child whose memories I cherish.

We had our favorite places to visit, and I felt the old excitement once again as I passed those same spots in my cozy car of sleeping children. At no other season do we hold more dearly to tradition than at Christmas, and I quietly rejoiced to see that in this world of continuous change I could still find a few welcomed constants – the star over a local kaolin company, what once seemed the largest Christmas tree in the world on the lawn in front of the EMC building, and the wreaths on the doors of homes.

That the traditional Christmas wreath is a circle is no accident, for circles represent continuity and infinity. I recaptured those timeless feelings during my private moments as I journeyed home. I remembered other holidays and late rides home after seasonal programs. I remembered the year I learned all the words to "Silent Night." I would sing the melody and my mother would harmonize as we passed the dark fields and woods along the dusty country roads that would lead us home. I recalled stopping along silent routes to gather pine boughs for decorating mantles and table tops.

I have many memories of car rides at Christmas but few of the actual programs that were my destination. It is the peace I remember and the warmth, the closeness, and the family intimacy of those journeys or excursions. When the seasonal din we create in our efforts to celebrate finally dies down, it is the peace that we cherish – the peace we were seeking all the time.

Christmas Simplicity

Santa and his sleigh probably didn't cost much. He was not more than four inches tall. His sleigh and tiny reindeer were white plastic, but when Mama put them in their usual place in the middle of the mantle, I knew Christmas must be approaching soon. My earliest and fondest memories of Christmas are not about elaborate parties or expensive gifts. The memories that remain and continue to glow warmly like the embers of a dying fire are composed of bits and pieces of moments that were probably not meant to be special but that held personal significance to me, sometimes, for unknown reasons.

I recall faces and events that were parts of my past. I remember family gatherings and the tingling expectation of the arrival of Santa Claus. Church programs, television specials, school parties on the last day before two glorious weeks of vacation, and rides through neighborhoods and nearby towns are all part of recollections I have pieced together and pressed firmly within my mind.

The weather was seldom agreeable. Christmas weather is unpredictable. It is balmy with hints of spring; it is cold and unfriendly, damp and dreary. I remember cold country churches made warm by the heat of ancient gas heaters where the men stood and talked among themselves as the women prepared holiday suppers and dressed the children in housecoats with dangling sleeves or tinsel-covered cardboard wings for the annual Christmas program.

Christmas cards arrived in profusion when stamps were less than a nickel and family visits were limited by the miles between us. The mailman came twice a day sometimes. We tacked cards around doorways and mantles, but not before we savored them over steaming cups of hot chocolate frosted with a plump marshmallow.

Finding the perfect tree was an important part of every Christmas, and some of my dearest memories are centered around pilgrimages through the woods around the homeplace. I remember going with my grandfather and, later, with cousins to survey dozens of evergreens in search of the one perfect tree. Holly, magnolia, and pine boughs were also collected to decorate mantles, hallways, and weathered urns by the front door.

The fragrance of Christmas is eternal. The pungent smell of fresh pine, the spicy sweetness of cloves and cinnamon, the musky fragrance of candles burning and fireplaces smoldering, the frosty perfume of wool coats still cold from the evening chill touch something deep within me that links all my Christmases together into one sparkling garland of emotions.

I have known many Christmases, and even though my life has changed between each one to bring me where I am today, the season makes me ever mindful of tradition. At Christmas I ponder who I am, and, for a while, the little girl, the emerging young woman, the mother, the maturing adult come together in the holiday glitter of Christmas present and in the gentle glow of Christmas past.

Christmas Recollections in a Country Church Yard

I could feel winter in the air as I pulled into the silent church yard. The sky was slowly turning into the fragile pink of evening, and the woods surrounding the building were as still as shadows stretched across the ragged grass that covered what had once been bare ground.

My mother had asked me to stop by on my way home and put Christmas wreaths on the old double doors. Services were held only once a month, but the church looked bare and forsaken without some holiday adornment.

I was in a hurry to reach home, supper, and a warm house, but when I started up the gray, peeling steps, I slowed my pace as memories surrounded me and the two simple wreaths I carried in my arms. I had not climbed these familiar steps in over five years, but ghosts of childhood and adolescence became real as I stood quietly before finishing my errand.

The church was locked, but I knew its interior by heart. It had been my grandfather's church, my mother's church, and my church. Attendance had dropped as families moved or members passed away. Only a few families had remained for the last several years, but finances and the harsh realities of business had forced these last faithful members to close the church with the exception of one Sunday a month.

Getting home was momentarily forgotten as I thought back to revivals when I was a child. We had two services daily for a week, and the church would always be full by Thursday night. The children would run among the parked cars after the night services while the adults lingered, their conversations rising into the warm summer air and disappearing over the nearby pine trees.

I recalled candlelight services at Christmas, Easter sunrises and breakfast afterward, baptismals and christenings, funerals and weddings. This church was a special part of my life, and even though I had begun attending another church, it would always be a part of me and my spiritual development. It was a part of my heritage, and I found myself gently adjusting the bows on the wreaths like a child lovingly straightening the lace collar on a special aunt or grandmother. I wanted the old church to look loved at Christmas. It was loved, I knew, despite the peeling paint and the slightly sagging front doors.

I walked very slowly and thoughtfully back to my car and to present reality. I left the silent, dark church on that cold winter's evening, but I realized that a part of me stayed behind. A part of me, I realized in the stillness of evening and in the recollection of memories made vivid by the hour and the season, had never really left and never would.

Season of Celebration

We called it Christmas weather – that season of unpredictable days in late November and December when gray skies hung heavily like a tired canopy and a steady drizzle made cool temperatures feel colder. We hunted Christmas trees in that weather, shopped from store to store for gifts, and ventured out of our warm houses to fetch another log for the fireplace or a scuttle of coal for the heater.

Christmas weather invites stuffy heads in school children. It numbs fingers and toes and makes noses glow like that of the fictitious reindeer. It causes cows to huddle together in pastures that have turned brown and brittle, and it teases with an icy whisper that blows away hats and pulls at scarfs like naughty children trying the patience of preoccupied adults. Yet, Christmas would not feel right without its traditional backdrop of wet and cold and gray.

Colored lights burn more brilliantly against the neutral tones of the season, and candles in window sills glow more softly through the mist that settles possessively over houses and their surroundings. Fires are even more appreciated when the soft drone of raindrops supplies the background for the singing of flames that wrap magically around logs whose burning defines the passing of time on a winter's night. What would hot chocolate with fluffy marshmallows or hot apple cider with cinnamon sticks be in any other weather? Also, Christmas sweaters and scarfs would only scratch and annoy the wearer in warmer temperatures.

I am tempted to think in metaphors when I contemplate this season of celebration so often heralded when the elements are the most uninviting. Although historically I know otherwise, I often imagine that first Christmas in a world of mist and darkness. I visualize the light from one small candle against the barren backdrop of a world devoid of hope and vision. Even though I know that our traditional depiction of the manger scene defies the actual event, I still like to think of shepherds and Wise Men gathering at the same time to complete the story that had been promised for so long.

I find it appropriate that we celebrate Christmas in our winter world. Christmas is its own season of light and warmth that sustains us even during our darkest days.

Christmas: A Season for Children

Christmas is quite near now. I have walked through malls decorated like the inside of a child's imagination. I have browsed through cozy shops that smelled of cinnamon and peppermint. I have sung the familiar carols and even exchanged a few gifts. My Christmas tree is blinking in its usual place of honor, and my old wreath hangs above my front door.

When I was a child, Christmas seemed so far from one year to the next. Childhood is but a flash in one's life, but to each child one year is a lifetime. Christmas, like birthdays and the seasons and other holidays, comes quickly now. We seem to stand still and watch the events that make up life come to us over and over like the horses on a carousel. January quickly becomes June. July speeds toward December. Another Christmas poignantly reminds us that another year is a memory.

Then there are the children – the children who open our adult eyes and enable us to see with excitement and expectation. I have seen a forest of Christmas trees in my lifetime, but to my children each new tree is still special. Decorating becomes a delight once again as I stand aside and watch my sons curiously finger each ornament and decoration hidden in tissue paper in boxes worn from years of use.

They are old enough to ask questions now. I find myself caught up in memories that come alive and sparkle in their young eyes as I tell them about the origin and age of my more worn but treasured decorations. I become acutely aware that I am the architect of their memories. I hope they will remember my stories and keep them alive for another generation of children.

The adult in me becomes weary of the extra activities and responsibilities that the holidays bring. The adult in me sees the sadness of this world more poignantly at Christmas. The sparkle of silver tinsel and brightly-colored lights contrasts sharply with gray poverty. The merriment of fellowship becomes too loud in the silence of loneliness. Christmas sometimes draws attention to our deepest fears and worries. Memories of Christmases past can come back to haunt us like ghosts when we hear the old songs and begin again the rituals of the season.

Then there are the children – the children who see life simply. Lights are brighter and candles glow more warmly to the child. After all, they have waited a little lifetime for the season to come again, and they greet it with complete joy as one who welcomes a dear friend.

Christmas is the season for children and for those with the child-like heart which believes in spite of poverty and loneliness. It is a season for memories and dreams, a time for revelry and reflection.

I watch the children – my own and others – and my spirits lift. The faith of the child, we are told, is all we need. Christmas makes that point so clear. Yes, the world seems dark at times, but what might it have been without that first Christmas and that special child who made the difference!

The Perfect Tree

There are two ways to decorate a Christmas tree – my way and the wrong way. For years I have decorated my trees alone because I have alienated family and friends in my quest for the perfect tree. In a world where perfection is often abruptly shoved aside, I hold tenaciously to one small effort at symmetry and order, and I decorate alone.

No one volunteers any more to go tree hunting with me. Step one in my yearly project is finding an evergreen that is shaped like those the Hallmark people draw on their cards. I have been known to inspect three-fourths of the trees in the surrounding woods or to cruise two counties, a half dozen supermarkets, and a dozen chain stores looking for that miracle of nature.

The perfect tree must be real, and it must have no funny side that looks as if a bear hibernated on it so that it must be turned toward a wall. It must touch the ceiling and be full enough to hold three large boxes of decorations. My search is a feverish one. Stock in major corporations is not bought with any more intensity than are my Christmas trees.

I can tell when I have come upon the tree that was meant for me. The clouds break, the sun beams down on me, and I hear strains of Handel's *Messiah*. Once the tree is found, I get it home and start step two – putting it up.

Perfect trees must not lean or wiggle in their holders. I have stuffed two editions of the *Atlanta Journal* into my stand to assure myself that my tree was standing as straight and steady as possible.

Finally, the fun begins. By this time only the staunchest of evergreen lovers is still helping me. I lose a lot of help in steps one and two, but often I am met with a resurgence of interest when the decorations are brought out of storage. The enthusiasm doesn't usually last, however, when I begin directing the decorating.

I firmly believe in equal spacing between tree lights. Also, some lights should be buried inside as well as around the outside of the tree. Never, never should lights of the same color be beside each other nor should burned-out bulbs be allowed to stay on the tree.

Ornaments should also be spaced equally from each other and must never touch. Clear ornaments should be placed near lights so that they might reflect color and shine brightly. Large ornaments should be placed on the tree first and followed by decorations of descending size.

I don't use garlands or tinsel. My nerves cannot tolerate garland or tinsel. I never could hang those silver chains in perfect loops and scallops from the top to the bottom of my tree. Besides, they always bumped my ornaments and threw my whole project out of balance.

Finally, the icicles go on. I admit I have growled at many helpers who showed no promise in icicle hanging. The important point to keep in mind when putting icicles on a tree is that they must be placed individually. I equate throwing icicles onto a tree with littering. One must carefully place each icicle (all 2,000 of them) across every branch until the job is completed.

The efforts I make are always worthwhile, and I love to sit and watch my creation twinkle and glisten in its special corner of the den. I especially enjoy sharing the moment with those close to me, that is, when they will speak to me again.

Christmas Tree Lesson

To call it a tree would be an exaggeration, but to my younger son, the pine bough that stands meekly in the sacred Christmas tree spot in our den is a mighty evergreen. If it were compared to a sentence, it would be a mere dependent clause, but it stands emphatically and will remain so until its replacement arrives next week.

He met me with it last Friday afternoon. He had that look in his eyes that every mother knows, that look that disregards common sense, threats, and rational explanations. He had cut it down himself, and he wanted to take it home.

I tried to explain to my earnest woodsman that the tree was small and weak and that I had, that very afternoon, just gotten my car washed and vacuumed. I continued by telling him that it was Friday afternoon, and I had no intention of getting down Christmas decorations and unraveling strings of lights when I had more urgent jobs waiting.

When we got the tree home, I suggested that it go on the deck. Homemade decorations might be fun. Lights and real decorations would weigh down the few scrawny branches that gave the little bough any personality at all. I would even help make some stars and a few candy canes. I got the look again.

The tree fit the stand better than I ever thought it would, and the icicle-shaped lights and miniature wooden figures did wonders for what had previously been probably the smallest tree in the forest. My son was elated. The transformed bough and a crackling fire completed a scene of peace and contentment in my previously uninspiring den. I had been defeated at every turn, but the victory was sweet, even to the vanquished.

At some point during our struggle of wills, I had begun to see the spirit of Christmas through the eyes of the child. My son saw a majestic tree when I saw a pitiful wisp of pine. My resolve to check off a list of responsibilities slowly crumbled as I realized that few holidays would remain when my children would want to create the magic that is Christmas. I gave in, not unwillingly, and the warmth I felt later in the evening by the light of an open fire and one lovely little tree emanated from within where the spirit of the season finds its only true source.

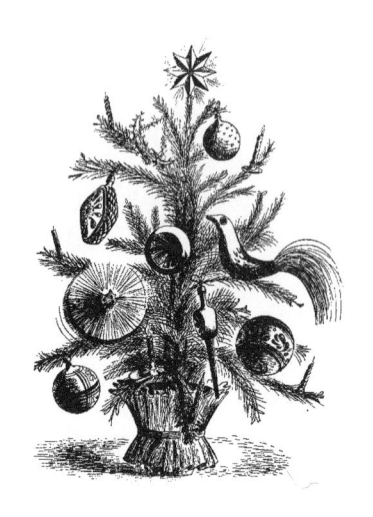

Timeless Charm

Our Christmas tree this year is cedar, not a special variety that is sold on vacant lots in the city or at grocery stores or nurseries but the kind that grows along fence rows or in pastures. It has a gap in the back and a few wayward sprigs near the top, but it touches the ceiling and fills one side of the den.

I love the simplicity of white lights, the charm of Victorian decorations that transport us to Christmases past, the elegance of trees adorned only in gold, and the nostalgia of wooden ornaments and popcorn garlands. Our tree portrays none of these ideas. We have no unifying theme, no trendy colors, no unique decorating effects. Our tree is a universal tree, an ageless evergreen that is the meeting place for Christmas past and Christmas present.

Bubble lights mixed with plain bulbs in all colors glow within the deep green branches. I was raised with bubble lights and cherish the ones I have been able to collect over the years. Their timeless charm mesmerizes my children as it did me and holds a place of honor on the tree every year.

Our decorations represent too many stories to relate in so short a space. I cherish the tarnished beads that hung on my mother's tree when she was a child. Precious, too, are the crude creations of my children when little fingers transformed simple objects into angels, stars, and snowflakes.

Some of our decorations were gifts to honor baby's first Christmas or a special event during a particular year. Some were gifts from students, friends, or family members. Some have no history in the giving but have achieved respect by virtue of their longevity. I have a box of retired decorations that look too worn to hang from the tree, but I cannot part with them just as I cannot alter the appearance of our traditional trees from year to year.

Sometimes I am tempted by the perfection of artificial trees, and I admire those works of art that reflect a creative spirit and a talented hand. I will forever have my live evergreen; however, it will always wear the worn decorations of my past, decorations that will be passed on to the next generation and, then, the next. Christmas is tradition, and my peace and contentment come from recreating the past and the best of its memories every year in that tree that is different but, reassuringly, the same.

Christmas Tree Memories

We decorated our Christmas tree last Sunday afternoon. The boys were more help than usual as maturity settles upon them gradually every year, but their enthusiasm continues to bubble from their childish innocence and makes the effort an adventure instead of a task. Christmas activities are steeped in family tradition, and no custom is dearer to us than decorating the tree.

The Christmas tree is the focal point of our den. We hang garlands of greenery over doorways, create a quaint village with a manger scene as its center on the buffet, and add live boughs of pine and bay leaves across the mantle, but it is our tree that mesmerizes us and awakens our imagination. Our tree is the image of who we are. It is always real. Artificial trees are lovely, but our tree must smell like winter and the holiday season. Our tree is always tall, so tall that it touches the ceiling and bends slightly until I carefully snip off an extra two or three inches.

The decorations reflect the years of memories accumulated by four generations of family members. Some of the ornaments are elegant – sugar plum coaches and crystal balls trimmed in gold braid. Some are wooden – pigs and cows that remind me of toddlers whose vocabulary consisted of monosyllables and animal sounds repeated at the gentle urging of proud parents and grandparents.

My most precious decorations are made of jar lids and pasta shells sprayed gold, clothes pins transformed into reindeer heads, and styrofoam stars strewn with glitter by little hands that are too quickly growing into manhood. Some of my ornaments belonged to my grandmother. A band of tiny angels will always have a place of honor on our tree. A brass bell, a drummer boy, a crocheted candy cane, and one tiny clear ball are reminders of another time when my mother, and, later, I were children decorating trees in other houses during other eras.

A Season of the Heart — 59

The tree is silently glowing in its place of honor. I shall sit when my hectic holiday schedule allows and enjoy the present as I remember the past. I shall enjoy the season and its surprises, but the sameness – the traditions that never change – will always be the most cherished part of the holidays to me.

No Carols the Second Time

The sky was blue, and a morning chill greeted me and my party of two as my sons and I bumped across a secluded field in search of our Christmas tree last year. My mood was as bright as the winter sunshine, and we were singing a familiar carol at the top of our lungs when we felt the bump.

A cloud momentarily hid the sun, and everything got very still as we stopped abruptly in the middle of a "fa-la-la." We were about to bog down in a patch of mud I had not seen because I had been so engrossed in my singing. I got out of the mud with a little luck, but I didn't take the hint and quit while I was ahead. Some days aren't meant to go well, but I didn't know yet that this one would be in that category.

We got our tree after much sawing and muttering from yours truly and took it home. Things grew worse. I could have picked any one of a hundred trees, but I had to pick the one tree that would defy me and three different tree stands. In short, the tree would not stand up.

I tried everything – chicken wire, bits of wood, newspaper, screaming and cursing. All failed. The tree would sit still for one teasing moment and then slowly fall over. Lunch time came and went. The afternoon shadows lengthened. My mound of tree stands and makeshift devices piled up in my den, but the tree refused to cooperate. Again and again it would fall. My eyes glazed over and my hands shook. At some point around mid-afternoon my sons quietly excused themselves and found diversion as far away from that cockeyed tree and their increasingly more insane mother as they could.

Dusk was settling in, and I knew my mind was going soon, so I tied my defiant evergreen to my car and left it to die in the woods. I felt no shame. It deserved no sympathy. As darkness came, I was sawing yet another tree just as I had been doing nearly eight hours earlier. Nobody sang carols this time. We got the new tree home and up, but I was too tired to get excited. Decorating the tree had, at some point during the day, become a challenge rather than a pleasure.

Finally we got all the lights on this more cooperative tree. I plugged them in and stood back to enjoy our overdue thrill, but I had relaxed too soon. For a moment my den looked like a scene from *Star Wars,* and then my lights went out ... and so did the microwave, the stove, and all the overhead lights on one side of the house.

My sons had been standing with me waiting for the effect. Without saying a word, they disappeared again. Insanity is not a pretty sight. When my husband came home, I was frying bacon in a small electric fry pan on the kitchen table. I knew when I was licked and had left the whole mess for him to straighten out. He didn't argue – something about the glint in my eye, I'm sure.

I haven't put up my tree this year. Oh, I've thought about it, and I will ... just as soon as I trust myself again with sharp implements.

Christmas Tree Obsession

Today is the first day of January, and my Christmas tree is still up. All of the other decorations came down last Monday, but I decided to enjoy the tree just a little longer.

I have this obsessive/compulsive thing about Christmas trees. The tree must be perfect, first of all. It must have a halo of light around it, and faint strains of the "Hallelujah Chorus" must filter down from the sky when it is first found in the forest (or the local tree farm).

Decorating this natural wonder must be done with the seriousness and the precision of a brain surgeon. Only in recent years have I turned parts of this job over to my children, but I watch with a careful eye lest two bulbs of the same color get placed too closely together or, heaven forbid, an icicle clump form at any point during the decorating procedure.

When the tree is finally decorated and the plugging-in ceremony out of the way, I begin my personal bonding with our creation. Each Christmas tree has its own personality, and the longer ours adorns one side of the den, the more reluctant I am to want to take it down.

I have even contemplated a year-round tree, but I feared that my sanity might be questioned. Think about it, though! Wouldn't the warm glow of tree lights at least through, let's say, early April be nice? Christmas ornaments could be replaced with Valentines and cupids in February and with bunnies and Easter eggs in March or April. By then the days would be getting longer, and the comfort of Christmas lights would be easier to give up for a few months.

The only hitch in my idea is dealing with a live tree. I water my tree. I talk to my tree. I send out warm, fuzzy feelings to my tree. My tree always dies within two weeks of its adoption and make-over.

The tree in my den right now has gone from supple to crisp in the last week. I am afraid to turn on its lights for fear of a spontaneous bonfire. It has also developed an attitude. Never trust a cedar tree, I say. Cedar trees are fragrant and lush at first, but then they turn moody and begin to droop. They bite and drop their brittle little cedar weapons into the carpet like tiny land mines that go off in your naked toe or heel long after the holidays.

My tree is coming down this afternoon. I am going to miss its warm glow tremendously, but I shall be on my guard. I have a bag to throw over it when I finally take it out the door. I hope it will leave without a struggle. Ending relationships is never easy, even when half of the couple has the I.Q. of wood.

Silent Night

The hour was late, and I was bone tired. My afternoon had been spent in an effort to mark off a few more gifts on my Christmas list and to finish other holiday projects. The pressure of numerous seasonal activities and deadlines was beginning to build up, and I had worked as one driven, ironically, to find peace of mind by pushing to complete as many of my responsibilities as I could during the day.

My bedtime hour had come and gone, and the rest of my family had already retired when I finally decided that I could end my activities for the day and get ready for bed. I sat down in the den for a moment while waiting for the bathtub to fill. It was then that I noticed the silence.

My eyes were drawn to the manger scene on the sideboard. It was surrounded by a winter village of ceramic houses that my sons and I had recently arranged. Two tiny deer were frozen in play beside a paper Christmas tree in the still scene. Carolers sang songs that I could hear in my heart if not with my ears. The lights from our real Christmas tree made the miniature world glow and glisten as it caught the reflection of colors blinking steadily in the darkness of the room.

I looked at the fireplace that was heavily hung with garlands of holly. Yes, stockings were hung there with care, and I marveled at how very soon two little boys would probably be giving up some of the wonderful magic of Christmas in exchange for the wisdom of the adult world that too often has little patience with dreams and fantasy.

I remembered again my weariness. It was not so much a feeling brought on by too much work as it was a frustration over what should be but too often is not. Christmas has become for many of us a season of madness rather than a season of gladness. I realized in the quiet of my den that few of us savor this special holiday. Too often we receive it in great gulps, never truly appreciating its essence.

I reluctantly turned off the tree. I did not want to break the spell that had settled so gently upon me. I could not help but think about the beloved "Silent Night" as I went up to bed. To many this lovely carol brings tears. Surely, memories are tied heavily to the emotions at this time of year, but I could not help but think that the inexplicable sadness that some feel as well as the compulsion to do so much are both rooted in our desire for peace. We need it, yearn for it, and actively seek it when sometimes all we need to do is sit and wait for it to come in the stillness and silence of an unexpected moment.

Christmas Music Charms the Savage Breast

Christmas music is the most diverse and the most wonderful music in the world to me. I listen all season to everything from Mannheim Steamroller's haunting version of "Carol of the Bells" to the Mormon Tabernacle Choir's quietly moving arrangement of "'Lo, How a Rose E'er Blooming." I listen to Christmas music year round, and I collect tapes and piano arrangements of every traditional and contemporary song I find interesting.

One of the duties of a conscientious mother, I have asserted, is to introduce her children to the finer things in life. Music is a very fine thing, I believe, and Christmas is the perfect opportunity to bring my nine-year-old and his eleven-year-old brother closer to the music of the season. My younger offspring, who thinks lyrics like "All around the kitchen cockadoodle-doodle-do" are truly stirring, and my budding adolescent, who thinks hard rock is the next best thing to pumped up athletic shoes, are suspicious of their mother's enthusiasm about "her music."

My children have sent out subtle hints to me over the past few weeks. Doors usually close quickly between us when I am in the thralls of the "Hallelujah Chorus," and my more aggressive younger son frequently asks me not to sing in the car when I burst into the chorus of "Angels We Have Heard on High." I remain undaunted, and my patience has recently paid off.

On a trip to Augusta last week, my young critics asked if they could purchase a couple of tapes of their kind of holiday music. The tapes were purchased, and as evening closed in around us, we sang (in three different keys at once) such oldies as "Santa Claus is Coming to Town," "The Little Drummer Boy," and every verse of "The Twelve Days of Christmas." My sons forgot themselves for a while, and as classics like "Dance of the Sugar Plum Fairies" and "Bring the Torch, Jeanette Isabella" rolled over, I was allowed to explain their origins. I was even allowed to sing snatches of other selections that have become standard favorites over the years.

The trip ended all too soon, and I knew that we had experienced a "Kodak moment" that might not be recaptured.

I still enjoy Robert Shaw alone, and "Frosty the Snowman" still beats out "Carol of the Birds," but I made a little progress last week. My sidekicks are pleased when they recognize melodies that were unknown to them before this holiday season. I may sing in the car now if I don't sing too loud, and I am allowed to play my tapes occasionally without a rumble from the back seat.

Music has a way of touching every one of us. To draw from an old adage, I might offer that you can lead a child to the classics and, sometimes, you can even make him sing.

Windows at Christmas

Located approximately 90 miles north of Paris is a cathedral called Chartres. It is not unlike many of its kind all over France – impressive in its aging dignity, awesome and imposing in its size. It is, however, particularly famous for the rose window that dominates the area above the entrance way. People who see it for the first time are usually silenced by its beauty; some even cry. Artists have tried to duplicate the intense blue of the stained glass, but they cannot produce that which time and the elements have created.

My mind wandered back to the singular beauty of that window when I began thinking about what I would say in a Christmas column. Everything has been said, so it seems. It would have been easy enough to rely upon the clichés and the verbal stereotypes, but the glow of that window haunted me.

Christmas is a complex season – a bittersweet interlude of intense joy for some and aching loneliness for others. It is a mixture of pagan revelry and theological reassessment. For some the story of Christ's birth is too childlike. Theologians and historians have argued the details and, yes, even the actuality of its occurrence for ages.

Not so many months ago I was verbalizing my beliefs to someone with whom I can say what I truly feel without fear of reprimand and ridicule. We were discussing the existence of a higher being. Life was not so pleasant at the time, and we found ourselves analyzing beliefs that we had held all our lives. I have always felt that if one's faith is strong enough, it can be questioned and scrutinized without any permanent damage to its foundation.

We talked about many aspects of our religious background, and one point among many that was discussed was the arts in religion. I find it personally difficult to understand how anyone can deny the existence of a higher being if for no other reason than because of the music and art that have been created to honor Christ. The most inspirational music ever written, whether it be the classic simplicity of "Amazing Grace" or the stirring power of Handel's *Messiah*, was created to praise the ultimate Creator. Museums all over the world have art work – paintings, statues, murals – carefully designed to provoke and stir the spirit of man and to try to express a universal longing.

To seek the concrete as an explanation for the intangible is a human weakness. To be bound to the tangible as an outlet for emotions and creative urges is also a mortal limitation. Yet, some of the most lasting expressions of the heart and soul have come to us through the arts, and the best of the arts has at its center a religious yearning and expressiveness.

As I hear the carols again this Christmas, as I view an artist's softly curving interpretation of the Madonna and child, as I enjoy the mellow glow of candlelight upon stained glass, I shall remember the simplicity and the majesty, the pathos and the power of a story that began in Bethlehem so very long ago. I shall be thankful, too, not only for the art but also for the Artist who created us all.

The Quiet Center

The Christmas season is upon us. Even before Thanksgiving, decorations were already being put into place on city streets and in store windows. I have already done most of my major shopping more from panic at not later finding certain designated items than from a desire to get into the holiday spirit early.

I have recently said at least a half dozen times that Christmas comes earlier every year, and I have heard the same cliché at least as many times. If we began this sacred season early for the right reasons, this world would be a better place, but Christmas begins before Thanksgiving only for commercial reasons.

I fear this holiday has become a period of controversy (Are manger scenes on public squares unconstitutional?), materialism (If I don't get Aunt Dearest an expensive gift, will she think I don't love her?), and stress (How am I going to shop, make cakes, plan the church Christmas party and keep up with my regular work?). The awe and wonder of the season have been replaced for many with tension and anxiety. The season that should bring peace has come to represent dread for those who have forgotten the quiet center at the eye of our man-made commercial storm.

No tangible gift can reflect the real love of family and friends. I wonder how much lighter our hearts would be if we gave the money we spend on gifts that usually go into closets and garage sales to a charity or to a worthwhile community project. Anyone who has given his time to a nursing home, a shut-in, or a hospital ward knows that by giving he receives tenfold. Wouldn't time spent doing for others be better than using that same time decorating the front yard and the entire house from attic to basement?

The true, spiritual purpose of Christmas will never be achieved by those who seek it with a flurry of activities and projects. The true meaning of Christmas comes only when we wait quietly and silently. Then only will it come and sit upon our hearts and minds to warm us like the steady glow of a candle, reassure us like the gentle face of the Madonna, and guide us like a star that has beckoned mankind to look up and to look within for the last two thousand years.

Commercialism vs. Christmas

Once upon a time in a land called America there lived a mighty and most influential king. He was quite adept in his art, so much so, in fact, that his subjects rarely realized the power he held over them. Indeed, they usually went about his work with zeal and enthusiasm. His name was Commercialism. This king was particularly powerful during one certain season of the year. He fondly anticipated Christmas, for it was at this time that he best manipulated his subjects. As the story has already pointed out, he knew his craft well because he appealed to his subjects in the name of love.

As he steadily became more successful, he proclaimed that his favorite season be lengthened. Thanksgiving became almost extinct because he had little to do with giving thanks. His was a much more self-centered rule. His campaign managers took full advantage of the media, and they understood psychology most admirably. Get to the children first! The chain reaction would be inevitable. Parents love their children; parents want their children to be happy. The astute ruler understood the bond well, and he used it to its fullest advantage.

Supply and demand became a challenge, and the game was carefully played. The ruler knew he had won when he observed thousands of his subjects nervously standing in lines in hopes of buying one of his creations, a baby doll with an innocent face and even a birth certificate to further the ruse. He smiled indulgently as he watched others looking in store after store for the miniature image of a brave warrior that would be but the first step in a chain of castles and accompanying figures. He was never complacent in his success. Every year he ordained that new inventions be sought to make secure and to further still his successful hold.

There were a few, however, over whom he could not completely cast his spell. These remembered another baby as the center of Christmas. He was a real baby, but He had no birth certificate save the prophecies of old. He, too, understood the power of love; He, too, was a king. We are once again at the threshold of the Christmas season. Which king will we choose to serve?

Dear Santa

Dear Santa,

Christmas is almost a reality again, and I have been thinking seriously about what I would like to have this year. I do not desire anything expensive, but I do appreciate durability. Something timeless would be nice, and even though I do not wish to initiate a trend of my own, I would like my gifts to be admired by others for all the right reasons.

I could certainly use some more patience. Mine ran thin several times last year, and I often found myself being too thrifty with the supply I had. I even lost it totally a few times for reasons both warranted and unwarranted. The new year will be filled with jars that refuse to open, children who refuse to behave, schedules that fail to be kept, responsibilities that fail to be fulfilled, and adults who act like children. A reserve supply of patience would also be a good idea for those times when I have a right to feel like blowing up a little. Patience is a lovely gift, Santa, and I have seen the ugliness its absence creates. Patience is especially beautiful on the faces of those who use their supplies well. I promise to use mine often, even when the object of my impatience appears deserving of my harshest words.

My thoughts bring me to my next request. Help me be more sensitive, Santa. A good dose of sensitivity, come to think of it, might be good in a lot of stockings around this old world. We have become so caught up in the process of living that we have forgotten about selflessness, quality, and depth of character. I need to be more sensitive in those forgotten areas. I put my best on display at Christmas and feel contented with myself, but I know that I need to remember that a smile on a gray morning in February or a word of encouragement on a dark night in July might mean more than all the holiday goodness I now lavish upon friends and family.

I want to be sensitive to what truly counts in life. With age I find myself sorting out feelings and priorities and discarding treasures that were worthless after all. Sensitivity does not come quickly, but I want to be aware of my callousness or of my apathy which can hurt as deeply as any directed abuse. Sensitivity is appreciation of moments life offers us as gifts from time to time. I know I have thrown away some wonderful moments in my ignorance. I want to be aware of the scent of spring flowers on the wind, children's unbridled laughter, silent tears, unspoken needs, babies' fingers, soft gray hair, insecurities masked as indifference, the special quality of simple moments that grow golden with age. I want to cherish more and judge less next year, and I need sensitivity to help me along my course.

Finally, dear Mr. Claus, I would like a good helping of enthusiasm. I know that the coming months will bring tired backs, head colds, boredom with necessary tasks, routines that seem unalterable, but I also know that my attitude about my circumstances counts more than the reality of what I must face. Enthusiasm can be infectious, Santa, so I hope you have stocked plenty this Christmas. I have not seen enough of it around lately, so I am hoping that you might have a surplus.

I know you are busy, so I will not keep you any longer. Don't forget, sir! Patience, sensitivity and enthusiasm are at the top of my list this year. I would appreciate all of them, but any would be fine. Even one of them could make a difference in my life and in the lives of those around me.

>Best wishes,
>
>*Virginia McAfee*
>
>Virginia McAfee

Saying Farewell

Santa Claus won't be coming to our house this year. I knew that my younger offspring was older than most who had dispelled their most precious childhood myth, and this year will be the year to begin many other years that won't quite be the same at Christmas.

Granted, the shopping was much easier with my sons' many requests, and I will be able to sleep all night without worrying about the alarm clock's malfunctioning or my children's hearing me bump down the stairs in the middle of the night. We don't need to put out the milk and cookies nor make sure that the fireplace is swept. We might even sleep a little later before opening the gifts that already sit in readiness under the tree.

I played Santa for many years after my older son was born, and now that his brother has crossed the same threshold that leads closer to adulthood, my job is over. It was a job that required creativity, time, and deception, but the pay was great. I shall miss my yearly pilgrimage to busy toy stores, and I shall especially miss the building excitement as Christmas morning drew closer.

I am sure that every adult lucky enough to have had a visit from Santa remembers when the magic disappeared. Oh, I know that even grown children expect some little surprise on Christmas morning, but when the real, heart-stopping believing ends, a cherished part of childhood goes with it.

Santa's magic ended for me when I discovered one of my dolls in the attic. It wasn't a new doll I was supposed to have received; rather, it was one that had been returned to the North Pole for repairs.

Each year my mother and I carried out a ritual of returning an old baby doll so that I might receive a new one. Under my watchful eye she would box up the worn doll, address the box to Santa Claus at the North Pole, and take the package to the post office.

I didn't know that the "North Pole" was just north of my head in the attic. I remember my confusion when I found one of our packages, but my initial puzzlement was quickly erased by some instinctual realization that Santa was a wonderful myth and not a real man. I had been trying for a year or so before my enlightenment to figure how one person — even a highly-charged magic one — could visit every child in the world in one night. Unexpectedly, I discovered the secret.

When we go to the theater, we accept the magic of the place and allow our spirits to soar freely by temporarily releasing them from the cumbersome weight of reality. The spirit of children soars because they believe in Santa Claus and the Easter Bunny and the Tooth Fairy; however, somewhere along their journey they cease to believe, not so much because they want to but because their knowledge of a sensible, ordered universe takes hold and makes them. My children made the transition rather easily because, unlike me, they have yet to realize how quickly childhood ends.